Internet English

www-based communication activities

Christina Gitsaki & Richard P. Taylor

OXFORD

UNIVERSITY PRESS

OXFORD
UNIVERSITY PRESS

198 Madison Avenue, New York, NY 10016 USA
Great Clarendon Street, Oxford OX2 6DP England

Oxford University Press is a department of the University of Oxford. It furthers the University's objective of excellence in research, scholarship, and education by publishing worldwide in

Oxford   New York
Athens Auckland Bangkok Bogotá Buenos Aires
Calcutta Cape Town Chennai Dar es Salaam Delhi
Florence Hong Kong Istanbul Karachi Kuala Lumpur
Madrid Melbourne Mexico City Mumbai Nairobi Paris
São Paolo Singapore Taipei Tokyo Toronto Warsaw

with associated companies in Berlin Ibadan

OXFORD is a registered trademark of Oxford University Press

ISBN 0-19-437226-X

Published in the United States by Oxford University Press, Inc., New York

Copyright © 2000 Oxford University Press

Library of Congress Cataloging-in-Publication Data
Gitsaki, Christina.
      Internet English : www-based communication
activities / Christina Gitsaki, Richard P. Taylor.
         p.   cm.
      ISBN 0-19-437226-X
      1. English language Textbooks for foreign speakers.
2. Internet (Computer Network) Problems, exercises, etc.
3. World Wide Web (Information retrieval system)
Problems, exercises, etc. 4. Communication, International
Problems, exercises, etc.   I. Taylor, Richard P.   II. Title.
PE1128.G528   1999
      428.2'4'0285--dc21   99-24460
                                                          CIP

No unauthorized photocopying

Editor: Chris Foley
Production Editor: Anita Raducanu
Associate Editor: Paul MacIntyre
Editorial Assistant: Maura Tukey
Designer: Tom Hawley, Hawley Design
Picture Researcher: PC&F, Inc.
Production Manager: Abram Hall
Production and Prepress Services: PC&F, Inc.
Cover Design: Tom Hawley, Hawley Design

Printing (last digit) 10 9 8 7 6 5 4 3

Printed in Hong Kong

ACKNOWLEDGEMENTS

Illustrations and realia by: PC&F, Inc.

Studio photography by: Rick Ashley

Pages 10, 11, & 12: Box shots reprinted with permission from Microsoft Corporation.
Page 14: The Celine Screen reprinted courtesy of Janis Riddle.
Page 34: Reprinted with permission from E! Online, LLC, Copyright 1996–98 (www.eonline.com).
Page 50: Courtesy of BBC World Service (www.bbc.co.uk/worldservice).
Page 51: Copyright Reuters Limited 1999.
Page 59: Mazda Miata image copyright 1999 Mazda North American Operations. Used by permission.
Page 64: Images copyright © 1998 PhotoDisc, Inc.
Page 70: Excite and Webcrawler are trademarks of Excite, Inc. and may be registered in various jurisdictions.

© Lycos, Inc. Lycos® is a registered trademark of Carnegie Mellon University.

The publisher would like to thank the following for their permission to reproduce photographs: Archive Photos, Image Bank, Miramax/Laurie Sparham/Kobal, Photo Edit, Stephen Fink/The Stock Market, Tony Stone Images, SuperStock.

The publisher would also like to thank the following for their help: Blue Mountain Arts, Indigo Restaurant, J. Crew, LookSmart, Richard Couture (The Coffee Net), Queen's University/The School of English.

There are instances where we have been unable to trace or contact the copyright holder before our printing deadline. We apologize for this apparent negligence. If notified, the publisher will be pleased to rectify any errors or omissions at the earliest opportunity.

CONTENTS

Scope and Sequence iv

Introduction v

Web Search Units: Organization and Features vii

UNITS

1   Computers Today 2
2   Surfing the Web 6
3   Electronic Mail 10
4   Famous People 14
5   Web Cards 18
6   Study Abroad 22
7   Eating Out 26
8   Shopping Spree 30
9   Watching Movies 34
10 Vacation Abroad 38
11 Cyber C@fes 42
12 Working Abroad 46
13 News Online 50

PRACTICE PAGES 54

1   Computers Today 55
2   Surfing the Web 56
3   Electronic Mail 57
4   Famous People 58
5   Web Cards 59
6   Study Abroad 60
7   Eating Out 61
8   Shopping Spree 62
9   Watching Movies 63
10 Vacation Abroad 64
11 Cyber C@fes 65
12 Working Abroad 66
13 News Online 67

TECHNICAL TIPS 68

Scope & Sequence

Unit	Identify	Basic Information	Basic Terminology	Skills Development	Skills Practice
Unit 1 Computers Today	Uses of computers	Computer hardware	Basic computer terminology	Practicing typing, cutting and pasting	Writing an introduction about yourself
Unit 2 Surfing the Web	Things to do on the Web	Internet FAQs	Strategies for searching the Web	Electronic trivia quiz	Comparing search engines
Unit 3 Electronic Mail	Ways of communicating	Free E-mail accounts on the Web	Parts of an E-mail message	Sending and receiving E-mail	Introducing yourself by E-mail

Unit	Identify	Prepare Your Search	Search the Web	Web Talk	Project
Unit 4 Famous People	Famous people and their occupations	Choosing a favorite famous person	Finding information about a famous person	Interviewing a classmate about a famous person	Creating a famous person profile
Unit 5 Web Cards	Types of greeting cards	Preparing to send Web cards	Sending Web cards to classmates	Viewing Web cards; classroom Web card survey	Making and sending greeting cards
Unit 6 Study Abroad	Reasons for studying abroad	Choosing an English language study course	Researching English language programs	Scholarship interview	Creating a school brochure
Unit 7 Eating Out	Types of international foods	Choosing a type of restaurant and food	Locating websites of restaurants with menus	Role-play: Ordering food at a restaurant	Creating a restaurant brochure
Unit 8 Shopping Spree	Ways of shopping	Choosing things to buy online	Finding items in online shopping catalogs	Discussing shopping experiences	Creating a shopping catalog page
Unit 9 Watching Movies	Movie ratings and preferences	Discussing movies and deciding on one to research	Finding information about movies	Interviewing a classmate about a movie	Advertising a movie
Unit 10 Vacation Abroad	Vacation preferences	Planning a vacation abroad: destinations and activities	Researching vacation information	Interviewing a classmate about vacation plans	Advertising a vacation
Unit 11 Cyber C@fes	Things to do at cyber cafes	Discussing cyber cafes and deciding on one to research	Researching cyber cafes	Interviewing a classmate about a cyber cafe	Advertising a cyber cafe
Unit 12 Working Abroad	Jobs and workplaces	Reviewing skills and qualities; choosing a job to research	Finding jobs on databases	Role-play: Job interview	Advertising a job
Unit 13 News Online	Ways to get the news	Reading and talking about a news story	Finding and reading a news story	Interviewing a classmate about a news story	Summarizing a news story

Introduction

Internet English is a WWW-based conversation course for pre-intermediate and intermediate learners. By using the Internet as a resource for the ESL classroom, it exposes students to real-life English utilizing the Information Super Highway.

This approach has many advantages. The Internet offers a variety of topics to satisfy a diverse audience; it is versatile in its use; and it is motivating. Through the Internet, learners are exposed to authentic language that is constantly updated. And finally, the Internet also enhances student autonomy by giving them the opportunity to manage their own learning.

Who Is This Book For?

Internet English is for adult and young adult students of English as a second or foreign language. It can be used with learners from pre-intermediate to intermediate levels of English. No advanced computer skills are required on the part of the student, as the Student Book demonstrates and explains the basic computer operations needed for the completion of the activities.

Why Use a Textbook With the Internet?

Without a textbook, learners are left to browse through information with no specific purpose. The Internet offers an abundance of information—but without navigating tools, learners can get lost in it. *Internet English* is a guide for learners as they independently surf the Internet giving them direction and motivation to complete specific tasks, have fun, and improve their second/foreign language skills.

Hardware and Software

Internet English has been designed to be used with any type of computer, Macintosh or IBM PCs (with or without Windows), that has access to the Internet. It requires the use of a graphic browser (e.g., Netscape, Internet Explorer), and word processing software (e.g., Microsoft Word, WordPerfect).

Structure of the Student Book

The Student Book comprises 13 units. The first three units introduce students to basic computer operations, the use of E-mail, and the Internet. These *Computer Skills Units* contain activities designed to help learners acquire the basic computer skills that they need in order to carry out the activities in this book. The remaining 10 units (4–13) are *Web Search Units* to be carried out using the Internet, E-mail, and a word processor.

Students who already have good computer skills can skip the first three units and start with the *Web Search Units*. Each *Web Search Unit* follows the same structure, which consists of four sections: *Identify, Prepare Your Search, Search the Web, Web Talk*. Each unit also has a *Practice Page*, found at the end of the book, that includes *Language Window, Computer Project*, and *Share Your Project* sections.

Finally, the *Technical Tips* (pages 68–70) provide a step-by-step explanation of how to carry out many of the basic computer operations required by the *Computer Projects*.

Lesson Planning

Internet English can be used in a computer-equipped or a traditional classroom. It contains enough material for approximately 40 classroom hours. This number may vary according to the instructor's teaching style and the individual goals of the class. It also depends on whether students conduct Web searches in class and whether the *Extension Activities* in the Teacher's Book are used.

A class using *Internet English* can be structured in a variety of ways. A sample lesson plan for traditional and computer-equipped classrooms follows. Both lesson plans assume 90-minute class sessions.

In Computer-Equipped Classrooms or Labs

Each *Web Search Unit* can be taught over two 90-minute classroom sessions.

Session 1. Students complete the *Identify* and *Prepare Your Search* sections. The *Language Window* is introduced and the writing activity given as homework. Students then use the computers for the *Search the Web* section.

Session 2. After completing the *Search the Web* section, students carry out the *Web Talk* activity. Students then use their computers to carry out the *Computer Project* and then E-mail their project to a group of their classmates to complete the *Share Your Project* activity.

In a Traditional Classroom

In a traditional classroom, the computer activities are performed by the students outside class time as an outside assignment. Each *Web Search Unit* can be taught over two 90-minute classroom sessions, supplementing Student Book activities with *Extension Activities* from the Teacher's Book.

Session 1. Students complete the *Identify* and *Prepare Your Search* sections. They also write down the keywords for their Web search. The Web search is given as homework to be completed outside the class in a computer lab, using a personal computer at home, or elsewhere. The *Language Window* is introduced and its written exercises completed in class. Students can also work on the *Extension Activity* related to the topic of the unit and outlined in the Teacher's Book. At this time, students can also be asked to print out some of the information and pictures they find in their Web search and bring the printouts to class for Session 2.

Session 2. Students come to class with the results of their Web search and they carry out the *Web Talk* activity. The *Computer Project* is then carried out as a classroom project. To do this, students may use the pictures and/or information they printed out from the Web. If the project calls for a combination of pictures and text, students may use scissors, paste, markers, and poster board to create the final product. They then post their projects in the classroom and complete the *Share Your Project* section with their classmates.

The Teacher's Book

In the Teacher's Book there are step-by-step instructions on how to present and carry out the activities in each of the units in the Student Book. There are also optional and photocopiable *Extension Activities*, as well as a list of useful URLs to support each of the units in the Student Book. The Teacher's Book also contains a set of photocopiable tests designed to assess language and computer skills.

Internet English Website

www.oup.com/elt/internet.english
The website has been designed to support the textbook and to be used by both teachers and students. It contains links to websites that work well with each of the unit activities, a teacher discussion page, and a keypal page.

We would like to thank everyone who reviewed the manuscript for their valuable contributions and advice:

Bill Acton	Marion Flaman	Victoria Meuhleisen	Tom Robb
Suzy Acton	In-Seok Kim	Sok Bong Oh	Jennifer Sakano
Kyung Hwan Cha	Jeong Ryeol Kim	Bill Pellowe	Anthea Tillyer
Steve Cornwell	Paul Lewis		

We would also like to thank the publishing team at Oxford University Press—in particular Chris Foley, Paul Riley, Karen Brock, Paul MacIntyre, and Mary D'Apice for their support and guidance during the writing and editing of the manuscript. We are more grateful to them than we can say.

Finally, we would like to mention our appreciation to our families, Dimos, Maria, Alan, and Phyllis, as well as to Mr. Maruyama at ASU, and Dr. H. Kurimoto of Nagoya, Japan, for their continuous support of our project.

Christina Gitsaki   **Richard P. Taylor**
Nagoya Shoka Daigaku   **Nagoya City University**
Nagoya, Japan   **Nagoya, Japan**

Web Search Units: Organization and Features

The first page of the unit introduces the topic with art and exercises designed to engage learners and promote idea exchange.

The topic of the unit.

There are four important sections in each unit: *Identify, Prepare Your Search, Search the Web,* and *Web Talk.*

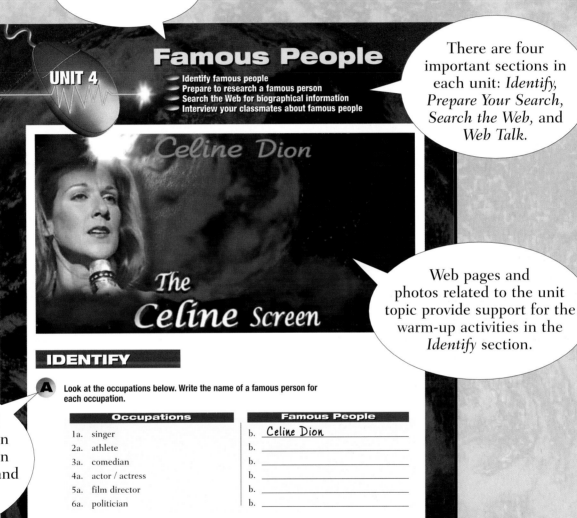

Famous People

UNIT 4

- Identify famous people
- Prepare to research a famous person
- Search the Web for biographical information
- Interview your classmates about famous people

Celine Dion

The **Celine** Screen

IDENTIFY

A Look at the occupations below. Write the name of a famous person for each occupation.

Occupations	Famous People
1a. singer	b. Celine Dion
2a. athlete	b. _____
3a. comedian	b. _____
4a. actor / actress	b. _____
5a. film director	b. _____
6a. politician	b. _____

B Compare your answers with a partner.

A: Can you name a famous *singer*?
B: Hmm, *Celine Dion*. Do you know *her*?
A: Yes, I do. OR No, I don't.

14

Web pages and photos related to the unit topic provide support for the warm-up activities in the *Identify* section.

The first part of the *Identify* section engages learners in vocabulary review and other warm-up tasks.

In the second part of the *Identify* section, classmates exchange ideas using a short model dialog.

PREPARE YOUR SEARCH

This section prompts learners to generate ideas that can be used in their Web search. It also exposes learners to useful vocabulary that they are likely to encounter while surfing the Web. Learners clarify their preferences, and by the end of the section they have a clear idea of what they want to search the Web for.

> A brainstorming activity elicits learners' ideas and reviews vocabulary.

> Here learners choose the object of their Web search.

> The last section gives learners a chance to talk about their choice for the Web search, and to hear about a classmate's choice. A model dialog and selected vocabulary items also help classmates exchange ideas and opinions.

PREPARE YOUR SEARCH

A Think of three of your favorite famous people. Write their names and occupations below.

Famous People	Occupations
1a. _____	b. _____
2a. _____	b. _____
3a. _____	b. _____

B Now choose one of the names above to research. Fill in the information below.

My favorite famous person is _____ .

(name)

He (She) is a (an) _____ .

(occupation)

C Now talk about your choice with a classmate.

A: What famous person did you choose?
B: I chose *Celine Dion*, the famous *singer*.
A: Why is *she* your favorite?
B: I think *she's* really *great*.

A: What famous person did you choose?
B: I chose *Princess Diana*.
A: Why is *she* your favorite?
B: I think *she was* really *beautiful*.

Words to Describe People

cool
handsome
beautiful
knowledgeable
great
talented
funny
skillful
wonderful
important
intelligent

15

SEARCH THE WEB

Search the Web guides learners through their Web search and helps them organize the information they find on the Web.

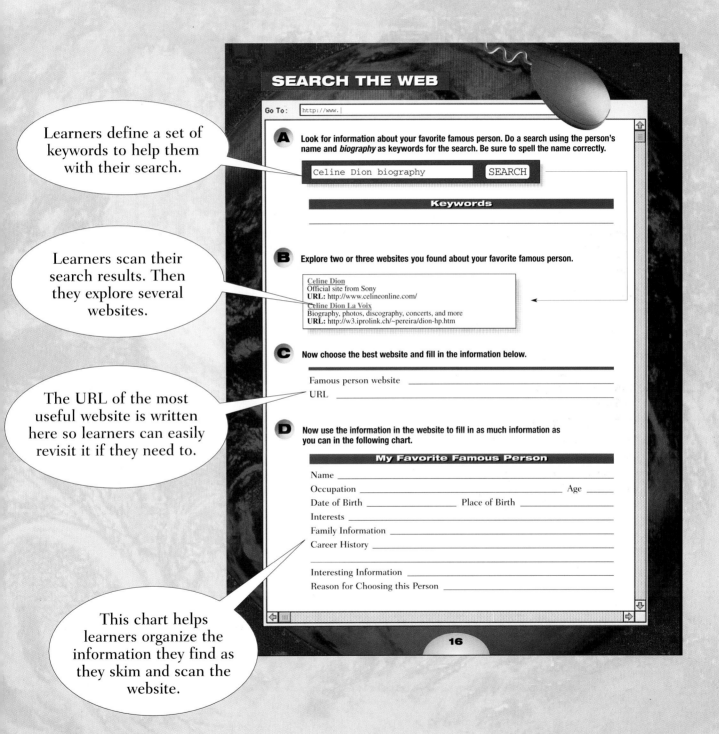

Learners define a set of keywords to help them with their search.

Learners scan their search results. Then they explore several websites.

The URL of the most useful website is written here so learners can easily revisit it if they need to.

This chart helps learners organize the information they find as they skim and scan the website.

SEARCH THE WEB

Go To: http://www.

A Look for information about your favorite famous person. Do a search using the person's name and *biography* as keywords for the search. Be sure to spell the name correctly.

Celine Dion biography   SEARCH

Keywords

B Explore two or three websites you found about your favorite famous person.

Celine Dion
Official site from Sony
URL: http://www.celineonline.com/
Celine Dion La Voix
Biography, photos, discography, concerts, and more
URL: http://w3.iprolink.ch/~pereira/dion-hp.htm

C Now choose the best website and fill in the information below.

Famous person website _____
URL _____

D Now use the information in the website to fill in as much information as you can in the following chart.

My Favorite Famous Person

Name _____
Occupation _____ Age _____
Date of Birth _____ Place of Birth _____
Interests _____
Family Information _____
Career History _____
_____
Interesting Information _____
Reason for Choosing this Person _____

16

WEB TALK

The last section of each unit is *Web Talk.* This section gives learners the opportunity to share the results of their Web search with their classmates and practice their English speaking skills.

A conversation task (interview or role-play) helps classmates share the results of their Web search.

WEB TALK

 GROUP WORK. Interview two classmates about the famous people they researched, and write the answers in the charts. Use the language below to help you ask and answer questions.

Questions	Answers
What's her (his) name?	Her name is Celine Dion.
What does she (he) do?	She's a singer.
How old is she (he)?	She's __ years old.
What's her (his) date of birth?	It's March 30, 1968.
Where was she (he) born?	She was born in Charlemagne, Quebec, Canada.
What are her (his) interests?	Golf, shopping, and collecting shoes.
Tell me about her (his) family.	She has thirteen brothers and sisters.
Tell me about her (his) career history.	She started singing when she was five…
Is there any other interesting information?	She does humanitarian work.
Why did you choose this person?	She's a wonderful singer and…

Example questions and answers provide a model for the conversation task.

Student 1

Name _____
Occupation _____
Age _____
Date of Birth _____
Place of Birth _____
Interests _____
Family Information _____
Career History _____
_____
_____
Interesting Information _____
_____
Reason for Choosing this Person _____
_____

Student 2

Name _____
Occupation _____
Age _____
Date of Birth _____
Place of Birth _____
Interests _____
Family Information _____
Career History _____
_____
_____
Interesting Information _____
_____
Reason for Choosing this Person _____
_____

Classmates use charts to write down each other's answers.

 Now look at your classmates' answers. Answer the questions.

Which of these famous people would you like to meet? _____
Why? _____

17

Here classmates review and discuss each other's answers.

PRACTICE PAGES

Each *Practice Page* contains three sections: *Language Window, Computer Project,* and *Share Your Project.*

The *Language Window* presents and practices language structures that are useful for discussing the results of the Web searches. The *Language Window* can be introduced before the *Search the Web* section or before the *Web Talk* section. It can also be given as homework.

The *Computer Project* gives learners a chance to use the information they find on the Web. They retrieve images and/or text from the websites they have visited and copy them to a word-processing file. They then edit the file in order to produce a specific project (e.g., a brochure, a profile, a poster).

Classmates share their projects, usually via E-mail. They then view and evaluate each other's projects.

UNIT 4 — FAMOUS PEOPLE: PRACTICE PAGE

LANGUAGE WINDOW

A. Look at these ways to talk about past events.

He **was born** on May 1, 1973.
She **went** to London **when** she **was 20 years old.**
He **graduated** from high school **in 1983.**
They **gave** a concert **last year.**
She **got married** two years **ago.**

B. Now write five sentences about past events in your life.

1. I was born in *(place)* _____ on *(date)* _____ .
2. I _____ when I was _____ years old.
3. I _____ in *(year)* _____.
4. I _____ last year.
5. I _____ years ago.

COMPUTER PROJECT

Use your word processor to create a profile of your favorite famous person from page 16.

For technical tips, turn to page 68.

1. Use one or more pictures from the Web.
2. Include biographical information and other interesting facts about the famous person. You may copy and paste text if you like.
3. Include the URL(s) of the website(s) you used.
4. Save the file as *YourName*.Famous.

Michael.Famous

My Favorite Famous Person is...
Bill Gates

Name: William Henry Gates III
Birthday: October 28, 1955
Country: USA
Town/City: Seattle, Washington
Nationality: American
Favorites: Computers and Family
Family: Wife: Melinda French
Daughter: Jennifer

SHARE YOUR PROJECT

A. Work in groups of three or four. Attach your famous person profile to an E-mail message and send it to the other members of your group. Write the name of the famous person on the *Subject* line.

B. Have a look at your group members' profiles. Answer the questions.

1. Which famous person profile do you like the most?
   _____
2. Why? _____

C. Share your answers with your group.

58

UNIT 1

Computers Today

- Identify different uses of computers
- Review computer parts and the keyboard
- Learn word-processing terms
- Explore and practice basic computer operations

IDENTIFY

 A Look at the different uses of computers below. Circle what you like to use computers for. Write down two more ideas.

Uses of Computers

1. send E-mail
2. write letters
3. do schoolwork
4. surf the Web

5. shop
6. play games
7. _____
8. _____

 B Compare your answers with a partner.

A: Do you use your computer to *send E-mail*?
B: Yes, I do. OR No, I don't.
    How about you?

COMPUTER HARDWARE

 A Identify the basic parts of a computer. Write words from the box in the appropriate spaces below. Then ask a partner to name the computer parts as you point to them.

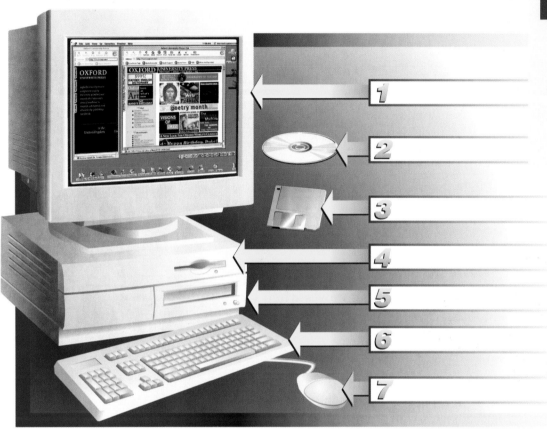

Computer Hardware

CD-ROM
Mouse
Floppy Disk Drive
Screen/Monitor
CD-ROM Drive
Floppy Disk
Keyboard

1. _____
2. _____
3. _____
4. _____
5. _____
6. _____
7. _____

B Answer these questions about the computer you are using. Then compare your answers with a partner.

1. What brand is your computer?

   _____

2. What is the operating system of your computer?
   ☐ DOS   ☐ Windows
   ☐ MacOS   ☐ Other _____

3. Which Web browser does your computer use?
   ☐ Netscape   ☐ Internet Explorer
   ☐ Other _____

4. How many buttons are there on your mouse?
   ☐ 1   ☐ 2   ☐ more

5. Does your computer have a CD-ROM drive?
   ☐ Yes   ☐ No

6. **COMPUTER LAB ASSIGNMENT.** Can you find these keys on your keyboard? Check each key as you find it.
   ☐ return (enter)   ☐ - (hyphen OR dash)
   ☐ space bar   ☐ . (period OR dot)
   ☐ shift   ☐ , (comma)
   ☐ tab   ☐ : (colon)
   ☐ delete   ☐) (right parenthesis)
   ☐ control (ctrl)   ☐ / (slash)
   ☐ escape (esc)   ☐ @ ("at" symbol)

A Match these word-processing terms with their definitions. Then compare your answers with a partner.

click   file (document)   cursor   window
highlight   ~~menu~~   icon   word processor

1. a list of computer operations	*menu*
2. a box on the screen that shows information	
3. a small picture or symbol	
4. text or other data stored together with a special name	
5. software for creating text files (e.g., Microsoft Word™)	
6. press and release the button on the mouse	
7. a little arrow on the screen that moves when you move the mouse	
8. select text/images with the mouse	

 B Now match these word-processing commands with their definitions. Then compare your answers with a partner.

New   Cut and Paste   Copy   Close
Print   Open   Save   Save As

1. duplicate highlighted text/images to put somewhere else	
2. preserve the contents of a document	
3. cut text/images from one place and put them somewhere else	
4. open an existing document	
5. create a new document	
6. send the contents of a document to the printer	
7. close the document without quitting the word processor	
8. save the contents of a document under a new file name	

COMPUTER PRACTICE

 A Open your word processor. Create a new text file and type the following scrambled sentences in the file. Save the text file as *Scrambled*.

A Day in the Life of a Young TV Actress

____ After dinner, I usually go to bed and watch TV until I fall asleep.

____ I'm out the door at about 7:15 A.M. and onto the dreadful freeway to work.

____ Following my bath, I catch up on some phone calls and then eat dinner at 9:00 P.M.

____ Work starts with morning rehearsal from 8:30 A.M. until 12:00 P.M. Then I go to lunch.

____ After lunch, it's back to rehearsal until 5:00 P.M.

__1__ I'm up at 6:30 A.M. I'm not a morning person, so this is *not* my ideal wake-up time.

____ From 5:00 P.M. to 6:00 P.M., we perform the show for the producers.

____ After the producers see the show, the executive producer gives us performance notes.

____ When the performance notes are over, I'm on the crowded freeway for the long trip home.

____ I get ready for work—I put on my make-up, get dressed, and have a quick breakfast.

____ When I get home at about 8:00 P.M., I like to relax in a hot bath.

B With a pencil, write a number from 2 to 11 in front of each sentence in the order you think is correct. The first sentence is numbered for you.

C Now use your word processor and follow the steps below to order the sentences correctly in the text file *Scrambled*. Do not save your work until you read section D below.

1. First, use your mouse to highlight the sentence you want to move.
2. Next, select **Cut** from the **Edit** menu.
3. Then, put the cursor in the new position and click.
4. After that, select **Paste** from the **Edit** menu.
5. Continue to cut and paste until you finish the story.

D When you finish ordering the story, select Save As from the File menu. Save the text file as *Unscrambled*. Print out the story.

E In class, compare your story with a partner's story. Are they the same? Discuss any differences.

UNIT 2

Surfing the Web

- Identify what you can do on the World Wide Web
- Find out about the Internet
- Learn some search strategies for the Web
- Take an electronic trivia quiz

IDENTIFY

 A Look at the list of things you can do on the World Wide Web. Which of these things would you like to do? Check ✔ "Yes" or "No" and add one more item to the list.

Things to Do on the Web

	Yes	No
1. meet people	☐	☐
2. get the latest news	☐	☐
3. order a meal	☐	☐
4. find a job	☐	☐
5. go shopping	☐	☐
6. make travel plans	☐	☐
7. _____		

B Compare your answers with a partner.

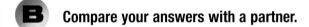

A: Did you know you can *order a meal* on the Web?
B: Really? OR Yes, I did.
A: Would you like to *order a meal* on the Web?
B: Yes, I would. OR No, I wouldn't.

INTRODUCTION TO THE INTERNET

 A Read the following FAQs (Frequently Asked Questions) about the Internet.

Internet FAQs

Q#1. What is the Internet?

A. The Internet is a network of millions of computers linked together by telephone lines, fiberoptic cables, satellite, and microwave connections. At the heart of the Internet is a high-speed network of supercomputers.

Q#2. Who started the Internet?

A. The Internet was started by the United States Department of Defense in 1969. It allowed information to move freely around a military computer network.

Q#3. What is the World Wide Web?

A. The World Wide Web, usually called "the Web," is the part of the Internet where millions of Web pages containing text, images, and sound from people all over the world are connected. A typical Web page looks like a magazine page, but with your mouse you can click on "live" areas on the page to go to a new screen.

Q#4. What can I use the Web for?

A. You can use the Web for research, business, entertainment, or personal interests. Some specific things people do on the Web are send E-mail, go shopping, find jobs, get the latest news, order a meal, and make travel plans. And the list gets longer every day!

B Now answer these questions about the Internet.

1. How are computers linked together on the Internet?

   _____

2. Who started the Internet? When?

   _____

3. What does a typical Web page look like?

   _____

4. What are some specific things you can do on the Web?

   _____

C Compare your answers with a partner.

7

HOW TO USE A WEB SEARCH ENGINE

Go To: http://www.|

A search engine helps you find documents on the World Wide Web. You tell the search engine what you are looking for by typing keywords in the search box.

To help the search engine find what you want, you need to be specific with the topic of your search. For example, if you want to buy a computer and you type *computer* as the keyword, you will get all websites that contain the word *computer*.

| computer | SEARCH |

Instead, if you type *computer buying guide* you will get better search results.

| computer buying guide | SEARCH |

There are also special operators, or symbols, that you can use to expand or limit your search.

 A Look at the search operators, example keywords, and explanation of the search results below.

Search Operators	Example Keywords	Search Results: Web Pages With...
(space) -	Chihuahua -Mexico	...*Chihuahua* but not Mexico
" "	"slam dancing"	...the **phrase** *slam dancing*
title:	title:France	...*France* in the Web page **titles**
url:	url:Sony	...*Sony* in the Web page **URLs**

 B Choose the best keywords for each situation. Circle your choices below.

1. You want to find out about wine, but *not* French wine.
   a. "French Wine"   b. wine -French   c. title:wine

2. You want to find Web pages containing the phrase *theme park*.
   a. title:theme park   b. Theme Park   c. "theme park"

3. You want to find Web pages containing the keyword *Tiffany* in the title.
   a. title:Tiffany   b. Tiffany   c. "Tiffany"

4. You want to find Web pages containing the keyword *goldstar* in the URL.
   a. url:goldstar   b. GOLDSTAR   c. title:goldstar

ELECTRONIC TRIVIA QUIZ

A Read the questions below. With your partner write three more questions. You shouldn't know the answers.

Questions

1. Who is the tallest man in the world?
2. When was James Dean born?
3. _____
4. _____
5. _____

B Think of the keywords you need to search for the answers to the questions above. Use any helpful search operators from page 8.

Keywords

1. "tallest man in the world"
2. _____
3. _____
4. _____
5. _____

C Do your search.

D Based on the results of your search, write the answers to the questions below.

Answers

1. Naseer Ahmed Soomro
2. _____
3. _____
4. _____
5. _____

E Compare your answers with your partner's. Then answer the questions.

1. How many questions did you answer correctly? _____
2. How many questions did your partner answer correctly? _____
3. Who finished first? _____

Electronic Mail

- Identify different ways of communicating
- Create your free E-mail account on the Internet
- Identify the different parts of an E-mail
- Practice writing and sending E-mail

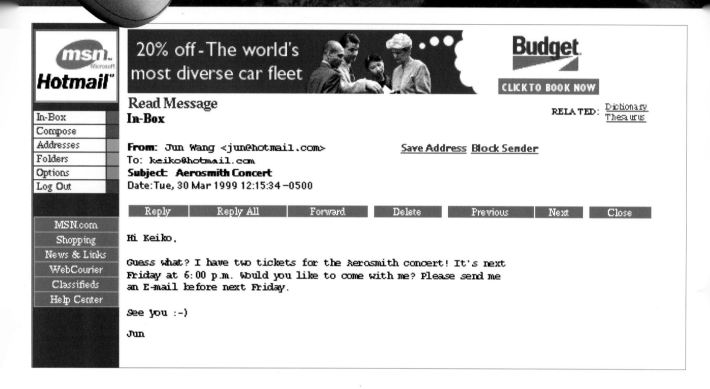

msn. Hotmail

20% off - The world's most diverse car fleet

Budget
CLICK TO BOOK NOW

Read Message
In-Box

RELATED: Dictionary
Thesaurus

- In-Box
- Compose
- Addresses
- Folders
- Options
- Log Out

- MSN.com
- Shopping
- News & Links
- WebCourier
- Classifieds
- Help Center

From: Jun Wang <jun@hotmail.com>
To: keiko@hotmail.com
Subject: **Aerosmith Concert**
Date: Tue, 30 Mar 1999 12:15:34 −0500

Save Address Block Sender

| Reply | Reply All | Forward | Delete | Previous | Next | Close |

Hi Keiko,

Guess what? I have two tickets for the Aerosmith concert! It's next Friday at 6:00 p.m. Would you like to come with me? Please send me an E-mail before next Friday.

See you :-)

Jun

IDENTIFY

 A Look at the different ways of communicating. Write how often you use each of these ways. Use words from the box or ones of your own.

Ways of Communicating

1a. write letters   b. _____

2a. talk on the phone   b. _____

3a. send a fax   b. _____

4a. use a video phone   b. _____

5a. send E-mail   b. _____

(almost) every day	
a few times	a week
(about) twice	a month
(about) once	a year
(almost) never	

 B Compare your answers with a partner.

A: How often do you *write letters?*
B: *Once or twice a week.* How about you?
A: *Once or twice a month.*

E-MAIL ON THE INTERNET

A Look for free E-mail accounts on the Web. Do a search using *free* and *E-mail* as keywords.

free E-mail	SEARCH

SEARCH TIP
Search engines usually offer free E-mail.

B Explore a few websites offering free E-mail accounts.

Hotmail
The World's FREE Web-based E-mail
URL: http://www.hotmail.com/
MailCity
FREE Web-based E-mail, available through any Internet connection
URL: http://www.mailcity.lycos.com/

C Choose a website and write the following information about it.

Website name _____

URL _____

D Sign up for a free E-mail account with this website. Fill in the registration form. Choose your user name and password *carefully*.

Hotmail Registration

msn
Hotmail™

Welcome to Registration for Hotmail, Microsoft's free e-mail service!
To use Hotmail, you need to sign up for a Login Name.

The information that you provide below remains private
This information is used by Hotmail for demographic statistics and to display the appropriate individualized advertisements. Hotmail keeps all of your personal information private and does not disclose it to anyone without your explicit permission. More accurate responses will result in ads that are relevant to you.

Choose a Login Name [_____] **@hotmail.com**
Only letters (a-z), numbers (0-9) and underscore (_). Login Name must start with a letter.

Choose a Password [_____]   *For secure access to Hotmail, your password*
Re-type that Password [_____]   *must be at least four (4) characters long.*

Your First Name [_____]   *Your Full name will be sent with*
Your Last Name [_____]   *all outbound mail messages*

E Write your E-mail address and password here.

E-mail: _____ @ _____ Password: _____

PARTS OF AN E-MAIL

Go To: http://www.|

A This is a typical E-mail format. Look at the different parts of the E-mail.

| Send | Save Draft | Attachments | Cancel |

To: jun@hotmail.com

Subject: Aerosmith Concert – Reply

cc:

bcc:

| QuickList | Spell Check | Dictionary | Thesaurus |

☐ Save Outgoing Message

Hi Jun,

B Put each E-mail term next to the correct definition.

To: Send   Subject: Cancel   cc:
Attachments   Message   Save Draft   Spell Check   bcc:

1. the main part of an E-mail where you write the information you want to communicate	Message
2. click here to send your message	
3. the line where you write the title of the message	
4. the cc line; the line where you write the E-mail addresses of other people you want to receive your message	
5. the blind copy line; an address here gets a copy of the message, but other recipients do not know	
6. click here to specify the file you want to send (attach) with your message	
7. the line where you write the E-mail address of the person you are sending your message to	
8. click here to save your unfinished message without sending it	
9. click here to cancel your message	
10. click here to check the spelling of your message	

C Compare your answers with a partner.

12

E-MAIL PRACTICE

A E-MAIL LIST. Go around the class and ask five or six students to tell you their names and E-mail addresses. Write the information on the E-mail List below.

A: Hi! What's your name?
B: Keiko, k-e-i-k-o.
A: And what's your E-mail address?
B: keiko@school.edu ("keiko at school dot e-d-u")
A: Thank you.

E-mail List	
Names	**E-mail Addresses**

B Put your classmates' E-mail addresses into the address book of your E-mail program. To save time, try to enter them as a group or list. Call it "Group List."

C Now send a message to the "Group List." On the subject line, write "My Introduction." Use the example below to write a short introduction of yourself.

Hi! My name is _____ and I am _____ years old.
I come from _____.
My interests are _____.

D Read the other students' introductions. Then answer the question.

What interests do you have in common with other students? _____
_____

Famous People

UNIT 4

- Identify famous people
- Prepare to research a famous person
- Search the Web for biographical information
- Interview your classmates about famous people

Celine Dion

The Celine Screen

IDENTIFY

 A Look at the occupations below. Write the name of a famous person for each occupation.

Occupations	Famous People
1a. singer	b. _Celine Dion_
2a. athlete	b. _____
3a. comedian	b. _____
4a. actor / actress	b. _____
5a. film director	b. _____
6a. politician	b. _____

 B Compare your answers with a partner.

A: Can you name a famous *singer*?
B: Hmm, *Celine Dion*. Do you know *her*?
A: Yes, I do. OR No, I don't.

14

PREPARE YOUR SEARCH

 A Think of three of your favorite famous people. Write their names and occupations below.

Famous People	Occupations
1a. _____	b. _____
2a. _____	b. _____
3a. _____	b. _____

 B Now choose one of the names above to research. Fill in the information below.

My favorite famous person is _____.
(name)

He (She) is a (an) _____.
(occupation)

 C Now talk about your choice with a classmate.

A: What famous person did you choose?
B: I chose *Celine Dion*, the famous *singer*.
A: Why is *she* your favorite?
B: I think *she's* really *great*.

A: What famous person did you choose?
B: I chose *Princess Diana*.
A: Why is *she* your favorite?
B: I think *she was* really *beautiful*.

Words to Describe People

cool
handsome
beautiful
knowledgeable
great
talented
funny
skillful
wonderful
important
intelligent

SEARCH THE WEB

Go To: http://www.|

A Look for information about your favorite famous person. Do a search using the person's name and *biography* as keywords for the search. Be sure to spell the name correctly.

Celine Dion biography   SEARCH

Keywords

_____

B Explore two or three websites you found about your favorite famous person.

Celine Dion
Official site from Sony
URL: http://www.celineonline.com/
Celine Dion La Voix
Biography, photos, discography, concerts, and more
URL: http://w3.iprolink.ch/~pereira/dion-hp.htm

C Now choose the best website and fill in the information below.

Famous person website _____
URL _____

D Now use the information in the website to fill in as much information as you can in the following chart.

My Favorite Famous Person

Name _____
Occupation _____ Age _____
Date of Birth _____ Place of Birth _____
Interests _____
Family Information _____
Career History _____

_____
Interesting Information _____
Reason for Choosing this Person _____

WEB TALK

A GROUP WORK. **Interview two classmates about the famous people they researched, and write the answers in the charts. Use the language below to help you ask and answer questions.**

Questions	Answers
What's her (his) name?	Her name is Celine Dion.
What does she (he) do?	She's a singer.
How old is she (he)?	She's __ years old.
What's her (his) date of birth?	It's March 30, 1968.
Where was she (he) born?	She was born in Charlemagne, Quebec, Canada.
What are her (his) interests?	Golf, shopping, and collecting shoes.
Tell me about her (his) family.	She has thirteen brothers and sisters.
Tell me about her (his) career history.	She started singing when she was five…
Is there any other interesting information?	She does humanitarian work.
Why did you choose this person?	She's a wonderful singer and…

Student 1

Name _____

Occupation _____

Age _____

Date of Birth _____

Place of Birth _____

Interests _____

Family Information _____

Career History _____

_____

_____

Interesting Information _____

_____

Reason for Choosing this Person _____

_____

Student 2

Name _____

Occupation _____

Age _____

Date of Birth _____

Place of Birth _____

Interests _____

Family Information _____

Career History _____

_____

_____

Interesting Information _____

_____

Reason for Choosing this Person _____

_____

B **Now look at your classmates' answers. Answer the questions.**

Which of these famous people would you like to meet? _____

Why? _____

Web Cards

- Identify different types of greeting cards
- Prepare to send Web cards
- Send Web cards
- Find out what Web cards your classmates received

IDENTIFY

 A Read the card messages below. Then match each message with a type of card.

Card Messages	Types of Cards
1. You're not getting older, you're getting better.	a. ☐ get well
2. Hoping you'll get better soon.	b. ☐ wedding
3. Good-bye high school! Wishing you a bright, exciting future.	c. ☐ Valentine's Day
4. Love makes all things possible.	d. ☐ graduation
5. Tiny child, sweet and new, the world is waiting just for you.	e. ☐ birthday
6. So the two of you are becoming one. That's one-derful!	f. ☐ new baby

 B Point to each card message above and ask your partner about it.

A: What type of card is this message for?
B: I think it's for a *Valentine's Day* card.

PREPARE YOUR SEARCH

A What types of cards do people in your country send? Check ☑ the types below. Then add two more to the list.

Types of Cards

- ☐ birthday
- ☐ good luck
- ☐ bon voyage
- ☐ new home
- ☐ congratulations
- ☐ get well
- ☐ thank you
- _____
- _____

B GROUP WORK (groups of 3–4). Prepare to send Web cards to the members of your group. (You will send them in exercise D on page 20.)

1. First, ask the members of your group questions like the ones below. Use this information to decide what type of card to send to each person (see the list above).

Example Questions

Do you have your birthday soon?

Are you going to take a test?

Are you going on a trip?

Did you just move to a new apartment or a new house?

Did you just pass an exam or test?

Do you have a cold?

2. Now write each student's name and the type of card you decided to send. (If the answer to all your questions is "No," write *thank you card*.) Then write each person's E-mail address.

Students' Names	Types of Cards to Send	E-mail Addresses
1a. _____	b. _____	c. _____
2a. _____	b. _____	c. _____
3a. _____	b. _____	c. _____

Go To: `http://www.`

A Look for Web card websites. Do a search using *electronic greeting card* as keywords.

> electronic greeting card   **SEARCH**

B Explore the websites and look at the electronic greeting cards of two or three sites.

> **Blue Mountain Arts**
> Send personalized animated electronic greeting cards by E-mail
> **URL:** http://www.bluemountainarts.com/
> **123 Greetings**
> Offering electronic greeting cards for all occasions
> **URL:** http://www.123greetings.com/

C Now choose the website with the best cards and fill in the information below.

Web card website _____

URL _____

D Select a Web card to send to each person in your group. For each card you want to send, you will be asked to fill out a form like the one below. Complete the form and send the card.

> Fill out the form below to personalize this card
> "It's Your Big Day!!" by Karen
>
> Recipient's name: Recipient's E-mail address:
> TO:
>
> Your name: Your E-mail address:
> FROM:
>
> *Click on Preview button (below) after entering messages:*
> You may click in the spaces below to personalize your card:
> Happy Birthday!
>
> *PLEASE SELECT MUSIC BELOW*
> ● "Rock Around the Clock" (Playing)   ○ "Happy Birthday"
>
> You may also enter an optional personal message here:
>
> ☐ Please notify me when the recipient views this card
> PREVIEW HERE before sending

WEB TALK

A Check your E-mail for Web card messages. Then go to the Web card websites and follow the instructions to view your cards.

B In the chart below, write the types of cards you received and the names of the senders.

Types of Cards	Senders
1a. _____	b. _____
2a. _____	b. _____
3a. _____	b. _____
4a. _____	b. _____
5a. _____	b. _____

C Go around the classroom and find someone who received each of the cards below.

Did You Receive...	Student Names
1a. ...a birthday card?	b. _____
2a. ...a good luck card?	b. _____
3a. ...a bon voyage card?	b. _____
4a. ...a new home card?	b. _____
5a. ...a congratulations card?	b. _____
6a. ...a get well card?	b. _____
7a. ...a thank you card?	b. _____

D Now report what you found to a partner.

UNIT 6

Study Abroad

- Identify reasons for studying English abroad
- Prepare to research an English course
- Search the Web for school information
- Interview a classmate about an English language program

IDENTIFY

 A Would you like to study abroad? Think about it, and check the best reasons. Then write down some English-speaking countries where you could study English.

Reasons for Studying Abroad

1. ☐ experience a different culture firsthand
2. ☐ make friends from different countries
3. ☐ communicate every day in English
4. ☐ go sightseeing
5. ☐ get a certificate
6. ☐ prepare for university in that country

English-Speaking Countries

1. _____
2. _____
3. _____
4. _____
5. _____

 B Compare your answers with a partner.

A: Why would you like to study abroad?
B: I'd like to *experience a different culture firsthand*. How about you?
A: I'd like to *make friends from different countries*.

PREPARE YOUR SEARCH

A Review the different types of English courses, social activities, and accommodations below. Then add more items if you can.

English Courses	Social Activities	Accommodations
Business English	go sightseeing	with a host family
English Conversation	go shopping	in a student residence
TOEFL Preparation	visit museums	
_____	_____	_____
_____	_____	_____

B Think of the English courses, social activities, and type of accommodations you would be interested in. Write them on the lines below.

English Courses	Social Activities	Accommodations
_____	_____	_____
_____	_____	_____

C Now choose the course you would like to research from the choices in exercise B. Then choose the location where you would like to study.

Course _____

Location _____

D Now talk about your choices with a classmate.

A: Where would you like to go?
B: I'd like to go to *London*.
A: What course would you like to take?
B: I'd like to study *Business English*.
A: Where would you like to stay?
B: I'd like to stay *with a host family*.
A: What would you like to do in your free time?
B: I'd like to *go sightseeing* and *visit museums*.

Go To: http://www.|

A Look for a language school. Do a search using *English, language school,* and the location you selected as keywords. Write your keywords in the box.

English language school London   SEARCH

Keywords

_____

B Explore the websites and study courses of two or three schools.

Angloschool
English courses for adults all year round, all levels in the UK
URL: http://www.angloschool.co.uk/
Leicester Square School of English
In London with three centres in the heart of the city
URL: http://www.lsse.ac.uk/

C Now choose the school you like best and fill in the information below.

School name _____ Location _____
URL _____

D Fill in the following information about the course you decided to take.

My School

School _____ Location _____
Course Name _____
Length of Course _____
Hours of Study _____
Social Activities _____
Accommodations _____
Cost/Fees _____
Reason for Choosing this School _____

_____

Reason for Studying Abroad _____

_____

WEB TALK

A Pair Work. **Interview your partner about the school and course he/she chose, and write the answers in the chart. Use the language below to help you ask and answer questions.**

Questions	Answers
What is the name of your school?	International School of English
Where is your school?	London, England
What course will you take?	Business English
How long is the course?	Six weeks
How many hours will you study every day?	Six hours a day, Monday to Friday
What social activities will you choose?	I'll go sightseeing and do some shopping.
Where will you stay?	I'll stay with a host family.
How much will it cost?	About £3,000
Why did you choose this school?	Because I like its English program
Why do you want to study abroad?	Because I want to get a certificate

My Partner's School

School _____ Location _____

Course Name _____

Length of Course _____

Hours of Study _____

Social Activities _____

Accommodations _____

Cost/Fees _____

Reason for Choosing this School _____

_____

Reason for Studying Abroad _____

_____

B **Now look at your partner's answers. Answer the questions.**

Do you prefer your school or your partner's? _____

Why? _____

UNIT 7

Eating Out

- Identify different types of international foods
- Prepare to search for a restaurant menu
- Search the Web for a restaurant menu
- Order a meal

IDENTIFY

A Look at the picture. Write down all the food items you recognize. Then write what countries you think they are from.

Food Items	Countries
_____	_____
_____	_____
_____	_____
_____	_____

B Compare your answers with a partner.

A: What's that?
B: *Tandoori chicken*, I think.
A: Where's it from?
B: It's *from India.*

PREPARE YOUR SEARCH

A PAIR WORK. Write a food item from the box or one of your own for each type of restaurant below.

Types of Restaurants	Food Items
1a. Chinese	b. _dim sum_
2a. Korean	b. _____
3a. Japanese	b. _____
4a. Italian	b. _____
5a. Thai	b. _____
6a. Indian	b. _____
7a. Steak House	b. _____
8a. Fast Food	b. _____

Food Items

spaghetti carbonara	~~dim sum~~
T-bone steak	kimchee
green curry	burger and fries
tandoori chicken	tempura

B Write down your three favorite types of restaurants and a food item for each one.

Types of Restaurants	Food Items
1a. _____	b. _____
2a. _____	b. _____
3a. _____	b. _____

C Choose a type of restaurant and a food item to eat there from the choices in *B*.

Type of restaurant _____

Food item _____

D Now talk about your choice with a classmate.

A: Where would you like to go for dinner?
B: I'd like to go to a good *Chinese* restaurant.
A: That sounds nice. What would you order?
B: *Dim sum...* I love *dim sum*.

SEARCH THE WEB

Go To: `http://www.|`

A Look for a restaurant. Do a search using the type of restaurant (e.g., *Chinese*), *restaurant*, and *menu* as keywords. Write them in the box.

| Chinese restaurant menu | SEARCH |

Keywords

_____

B Explore the websites of two or three restaurants.

Buffet Dynasty
Serving authentic Chinese food seven days a week
URL: http://www.charlottenet.com/rest/bdynasty/index.htm
Great Wall of China
Includes menu
URL: http://www.contentpark.com/greatwall/

C Now choose the restaurant you like best and fill in the information below. Make sure there is a menu on the restaurant's website.

Restaurant name _____

City and country _____

URL _____

D Look at your restaurant's menu and choose the items you would like to order. Write your choices below.

Menu Items

Appetizers/Starters _____

Main Courses _____

Desserts _____

Beverages _____

E Print out the menu.

WEB TALK

A ROLE-PLAY. **Act out a restaurant scene. One student plays the customer, and the other plays the waiter. Before starting, the customer gives a copy of the restaurant menu he/she found on the Web to the waiter to use in the role-play.**

Waiter	Customer
Show the customer to a table and give him/her a copy of the menu. Write the order on the check at the bottom of the page. Fill in the prices and total and give the check to the customer after dinner. Use the language below to help you take the customer's order.	After the waiter seats you, look at the menu and order the meal you selected. Ask for the check at the end of the meal. Use the language below to help you tell the waiter what you want.

Waiter	Customer
Are you ready to order?	Yes. Not quite yet. Could we have a little more time?
What would you like for an appetizer?	I'll have the sharkfin soup.
What would you like for the main course?	I'd like the spicy shrimp.
Would you like anything to drink?	Yes, I'd like some tea. No, thank you. Just water.
Would you like a salad?	Yes, please. No, thank you.
Can I get you anything else?	Yes, what do you have for dessert? No, thanks. Just the check, please.

Guest Check

DATE	PERSONS	CHECK NUMBER
		78304

	$
TAX	
TOTAL	

 B **Now change roles and perform the role-play again.**

UNIT 8

Shopping Spree

- Identify different ways of shopping
- Prepare to buy three items on-line
- Search for online shopping websites
- Talk about your shopping experience

jcrew.com

Home   Help   Order by Item#   View Order   Checkout

MEN'S   WOMEN'S   DIRECTORY   CLEARANCE   WEEKLY SALE   BACK ISSUES   FUN STUFF   AFFILIATE NETWORK

Cargos $38   V-neck $16   Drawstring cargos $38

Spring to Summer

Men's
Shirts
Polos, tees
Pants
Sweaters, outerwear
Shorts, swim
J.Crew golf
Sport
Underwear, sleepwear
Shoes, accessories

Women's
Classic suiting shirts
Shirts
Spring sweaters
Tees
Shorts, pants
Skirts, dresses
Swimwear
Intimates
Shoes, accessories

IDENTIFY

A Look at the ways to shop below. Write down some things you would buy using each of these ways.

Ways to Shop	Things to Buy
1a. from a mail-order catalog	b. _____
2a. at a store	b. _____
3a. from a TV home shopping program	b. _____
4a. through an online catalog	b. _____
5a. from a door-to-door salesperson	b. _____

B Compare your answers with a partner.

A: What would you buy *from a mail-order catalog?*
B: I'd probably buy *clothes* or *CDs.* How about you?
A: I might buy *shoes* or *jewelry.*

A Read the lists of items you can buy online. Then add three items to each list.

Clothes and Accessories	Sports and Fitness Equipment	Electronic Equipment
jeans	inline skates	personal computer
T-shirt	soccer ball	alarm clock
sunglasses	skis	television
watch	snowboard	cell phone
_____	_____	_____
_____	_____	_____
_____	_____	_____

B Write one item you would like to buy online for each of the categories below. Then write the price you would like to pay.

Clothes and Accessories

Item _____ Price _____

Sports and Fitness Equipment

Item _____ Price _____

Electronic Equipment

Item _____ Price _____

C Now talk about your choices with a classmate.

A: What *clothes and accessories* would you like to buy?
B: I'm looking for *jeans*.
A: How much would you like to pay?
B: About *50 dollars*.

Go To: http://www.|

A Look for shopping catalogs online. Do separate searches using *shopping* and each of the items (e.g., *jeans)* you want to buy as keywords. Write your keywords in the box.

shopping jeans   SEARCH

SEARCH TIP
You may also try the shopping links on your favorite search engine.

Keywords

1. _____ 2. _____ 3. _____

B Explore websites for each of the items you want to buy.

Texas Jeans
URL: http://www.texasjeans.com/
Underground Jeans
URL: http://www.undergroundjeans.com/
Excite Shopping: Clothes&Beauty: Jeans
URL: http://www.excite.com/shopping/clothes_and_beauty/jeans/

C Now choose websites from which you would like to order each of the items on your list. Fill in the information below. Make sure the websites list the prices of the items.

Item	Company Name	URL
_____	_____	_____
_____	_____	_____
_____	_____	_____

D Find the things you want to buy. Fill in the following information about your shopping.

Clothes and   Item _____
Accessories   Brand Name _____ Price _____

Sports and Fitness   Item _____
Equipment   Brand Name _____ Price _____

Electronic   Item _____
Equipment   Brand Name _____ Price _____

WEB TALK

A Ask three classmates about their shopping experience, and write the answers in the charts. Use the language below to help you ask and answer questions.

Questions	Answers
What companies' websites did you visit?	J.Crew and Gucci.
What did you buy?	I bought a pair of jeans, a watch…
How much did you spend?	I spent US$325.
How did you pay?	I paid by credit card.

Student A _____

Websites _____

_____

_____

Shopping List _____

_____

_____

Total Cost _____

Method of Payment _____

Student B _____

Websites _____

_____

_____

Shopping List _____

_____

_____

Total Cost _____

Method of Payment _____

Student C _____

Websites _____

_____

_____

Shopping List _____

_____

_____

Total Cost _____

Method of Payment _____

J.Crew sport

Logo tees   Tees, tank, sweats   Jackets, pants, shorts

B Look at your classmates' answers. Answer the question.

Who spent the most money? _____

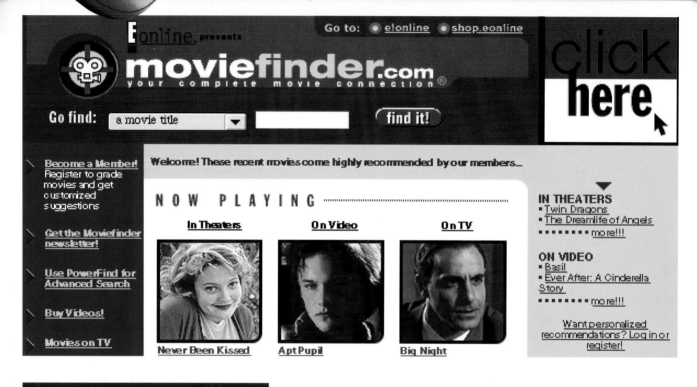

Watching Movies

me preferences
- Prepare to preview movies
- Search the Web for movie information
- Interview a classmate about a movie

IDENTIFY

 A List some movies that you have seen recently and rate each one.

Movies	My Rating	Ratings Chart
1a. Titanic	b. ☆☆☆☆☆	☆☆☆☆☆ I loved it!
2a. _____	b. _____	☆☆☆☆ I enjoyed it.
3a. _____	b. _____	☆☆☆ It was OK.
4a. _____	b. _____	☆☆ I didn't like it that much.
5a. _____	b. _____	☆ I hated it.

 B Talk to your partner about the movies.

A: Have you seen any movies lately?
B: Yes. I rented *Titanic*. / saw *Titanic* at the movies.
A: Really? What did you think of it?
B: *I loved it!*

PREPARE YOUR SEARCH

A Think of a movie for each type below. Then write a word from the box, or one of your own words, to describe the movie.

Type	Movie	Description	Words to Describe Movies
1. love story	Titanic	romantic	sad
2. action movie			funny
3. science-fiction movie			exciting
			weird
4. horror movie			interesting
			boring
5. comedy			romantic
6. animated movie			scary
			violent

B Write down three movies you would like to see. What types of movies are they?

Movies	Types
1a. _____	b. _____
2a. _____	b. _____
3a. _____	b. _____

C Now choose the movie you would most like to see this weekend. Fill in the information below.

Name of movie _____

Type of movie _____

D Now talk about your choice with a classmate.

A: What kind of movie would you like to see this weekend?
B: I'd like to see *Titanic*.
A: What type of movie is it?
B: It's a *love story*.
A: How would you describe it?
B: It's *romantic*.

Go To: `http://www.`

A Look for movie databases. Use *movie database* as keywords. Inside the database, use the title of your movie as keywords.

```
movie database                          SEARCH
```

B Explore two or three different movie databases.

Internet Movie Database
URL: http://www.imdb.com/
All Movie Guide
URL: http://www.allmovie.com/
Motion Picture Database
URL: http://www.tvguide.com/movies/mopic/cgi-bin/page.c

C Fill in the information about the movie you would like to see.

Movie title _____

URL _____

D Read the information about the movie, and fill in as many items as you can in the following chart.

My Movie Choice

Movie Title _____

Type _____

Date of Release _____

Stars _____

Director _____

Film Company _____

Plot Summary (Story) _____

_____

Setting _____

Special Effects/Computer Graphics _____

Other Information _____

Reason for Choosing This Movie _____

WEB TALK

A   PAIR WORK. Interview your partner about the movie he/she chose, and write the answers in the chart. Use the language below to help you ask and answer questions.

Questions	Answers
What's the title of the movie?	*Titanic*
What type of movie is it?	It's a love story.
What's the date of release?	December 19, 1997
Who are the stars?	Leonardo Di Caprio, Kate Winslet,...
Who is the director?	James Cameron
What's the film company?	Paramount Pictures and 20th Century Fox
What's the movie about?	Two people fall in love on...
What's the setting?	An oceangoing passenger ship in 1912
Are there any special effects or computer graphics?	Yes, there are a lot of computer graphics.
What other information can you tell me?	It won the Academy Award for Best Picture...
Why did you choose this movie?	Because I heard it's a great movie.

My Partner's Movie Choice

Movie Title _____

Type _____

Date of Release _____

Stars _____

Director _____

Film Company _____

Plot Summary (Story) _____

_____

Setting _____

Special Effects/Computer Graphics _____

Other Information _____

Reason for Choosing This Movie _____

B   Now look your partner's answers. Answer the questions.

Do you prefer your movie or your partner's? _____

Why? _____

Vacation Abroad

UNIT 10
- Identify your classmates' vacation preferences
- Prepare to research a vacation
- Search the Web for vacation information
- Interview a classmate about vacation plans

IDENTIFY

First complete the questions below about vacation preferences. Then go around the class and find someone who answers "yes" to each question. Write their names in the box.

Questions	Student Names
1. …sometimes goes abroad. Do you _sometimes go abroad_ ?	_____
2. …enjoys travelling by plane. Do you _____ ?	_____
3. …enjoys travelling by train. Do you _____ ?	_____
4. …likes adventure tours. Do you _____ ?	_____
5. …likes tropical vacations. Do you _____ ?	_____

A PAIR WORK. Work with a partner to write a vacation destination for each activity.

Vacation Destinations	Activities
1a. _Australia_	b. scuba diving
2a. _____	b. safari
3a. _____	b. mountain climbing
4a. _____	b. fishing
5a. _____	b. surfing
6a. _____	b. skiing / snowboarding
7a. _____	b. whale watching

B Write down three vacation destinations you would like to visit and one activity for each. Choose from the list above or use your own ideas.

Vacation Destinations	Activities
1a. _____	b. _____
2a. _____	b. _____
3a. _____	b. _____

C Now choose one vacation destination to research and the activity you would like to do there.

Destination _____

Activity _____

D Now talk about your choices with a classmate.

A: Where would you like to go for your vacation?
B: I'd like to go to *Australia*.
A: That sounds great. What would you like to do there?
B: I'd like to go *scuba diving*.

Go To: `http://www.`

A Look for vacation information. Do a search using the destination you've chosen, the type of activity, and *accommodation* as keywords. Write your keywords in the box.

> Australia diving accommodation   SEARCH

SEARCH TIP
You can also try the travel information and package tours in your favorite search engine.

Keywords

_____

B Explore the vacation websites you found.

Holiday North Queensland
For your travel ideas including accommodations
URL: http://www.holidaynq.com.au/
Cairns Connect
Guide includes hotels, reef tours, restaurants, scuba diving
URL: http://www.cairnsconnect.com/

C Now choose the vacation website you like best and fill in the information below.

Vacation website _____

URL _____

D Fill in as much of the information as you can in the chart.

My Vacation Plan

Destination: _____ Dates: from _____ to _____

Accommodations: Type _____

                  Name _____

                  Number of Nights _____ Cost _____

                  Facilities _____

Activities: _____

_____

Other Information: Special Attractions, Tours _____

                   Weather _____

Reason for Choosing This Vacation: _____

WEB TALK

A PAIR WORK. Interview your partner about the vacation he/she chose, and write the answers in the chart. Use the language below to help you ask and answer questions.

Questions	Answers
Where will you go?	I'll go to Cairns, Australia.
What are the dates of your stay?	From August 1st to August 15th
What type of accommodations will you choose?	I'll stay at a resort hotel.
What's the name?	The Island Queen
How many nights will you stay there?	Four nights
How much will it cost?	AU$560
What facilities do they have?	They have large rooms, tennis courts, …
What will you do there?	I'll go diving on the Great Barrier Reef.
Are there any special attractions or tours?	They have an interesting rainforest tour.
How is the weather there?	It's hot and humid.
Why did you choose this vacation?	Because I want to try diving and…

My Partner's Vacation Plan

Destination: _____ Dates: from _____ to _____

Accommodations: Type _____

Name _____

Number of Nights _____ Cost _____

Facilities _____

Activities: _____

_____

Other Information: Special Attractions, Tours _____

Weather _____

Reason for Choosing This Vacation: _____

B Now look at your partner's answers. Answer the questions.

Do you prefer your vacation or your partner's? _____

Why? _____

41

Cyber C@fes

UNIT 11

- Identify things you can do at a cyber cafe
- Prepare to search for cyber cafes
- Search the Web for cyber cafes in different countries
- Interview a classmate about a cyber cafe

A cyber cafe is a coffee shop with computers connected to the Internet.
For a small fee, you can surf the Web and use E-mail.

IDENTIFY

A Look at the list of things you can do at a cyber cafe. Check ☑ the ones that you would do.

Things to Do at a Cyber Cafe

1. ☐ surf the Web
2. ☐ send or check E-mail
3. ☐ play computer games
4. ☐ eat a sandwich
5. ☐ drink cappuccino
6. ☐ listen to pop music

B Compare your answers with a partner.

A: What would you do at a cyber cafe?
B: I would *drink cappuccino* and *surf the Web*. How about you?
A: I would *listen to pop music* and *check my E-mail*.

PREPARE YOUR SEARCH

A Look at the chart of things you can do at a cyber cafe. Add your ideas to the spaces. Then compare your ideas with a partner.

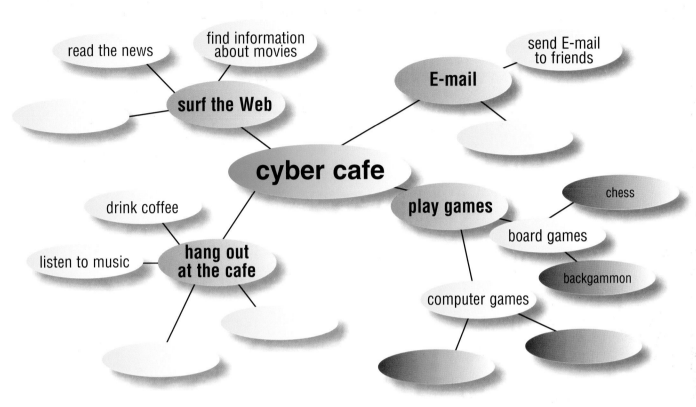

B Write down the three things you would most like to do at a cyber cafe.

I would like to...
1. _____
2. _____
3. _____

C Choose a country where you would like to find a cyber cafe.

Country _____

D Now talk about your choice with a classmate.

A: In which country would you like to find a cyber cafe?
B: I'd like to find a cyber cafe in *England*.
A: What would you do there?
B: I'd probably *check my E-mail, read the news,* and *have a snack*.

SEARCH THE WEB

Go To: `http://www.`

A Look for a cyber cafe in the country you have chosen. Search the Web using *cyber cafe* or *Internet cafe* and the name of the country as keywords. Write your keywords in the box.

| cyber cafe England | SEARCH |

Keywords

1. _____   2. _____

B Explore the websites of two or three cyber cafes in the country you have chosen.

C@fe.net
URL: http://www.cafenet.uk.com
Intercafe
Tapping into the World Wide Web is just the beginning
URL: http://www.intercafe.co.uk/
World Cafe
URL: http://www.worldcafe.smallplanet.co.uk/

C Now choose the cyber cafe that interests you the most. Fill in the information below.

Cyber cafe _____   URL _____

D Fill in as much of the information below as you can about the cyber cafe you chose.

My Cyber Cafe

Name _____ Location _____

Business Hours _____

Internet Connection Cost _____

Food _____

Drinks _____

Hardware _____

Software _____

Computer Games _____

Training _____

Other _____

WEB TALK

A PAIR WORK. Interview your partner about the cyber cafe he/she researched, and write the answers in the chart. Use the language below to help you ask and answer questions.

Questions	Answers
What's the name of the cyber cafe?	It's called Cafe Connect.
Where is it?	It's in London.
When are they open?	They're open from 8:00 A.M. to 11:00 P.M.
How much does the Internet connection cost?	It costs £4.80 per hour.
What kinds of food do they serve?	They serve mostly sandwiches and desserts.
What kinds of drinks do they have?	They have cappuccino, tea, juice…
Tell me about their hardware?	They have Apple Macintosh computers…
What games do they have?	Starsiege, Quark II, Half-life…
Do they offer any training or classes?	Yes, they offer classes in Web page design.
What else do they offer?	They have a gift shop.

My Partner's Cyber Cafe

Name _____ Location _____

Business Hours _____

Internet Connection Cost _____

Food _____

Drinks _____

Hardware _____

Software _____

Computer Games _____

Training _____

Other _____

B Now look your partner's answers. Answer the questions.

Do you prefer your cyber cafe or your partner's? _____

Why? _____

Working Abroad

- Identify different types of jobs and workplaces
- Prepare to find a job in another country
- Search the Web for jobs
- Role-play a job interview

IDENTIFY

 A Match the jobs on the left with the workplaces on the right.

Jobs	Workplaces
1. ☐ ski instructor	a. at beaches and swimming pools
2. ☐ nanny	b. at Alpine resorts
3. ☐ camp counselor	c. in private homes
4. ☐ language teacher	d. in restaurant kitchens
5. ☐ cook	e. at summer camps
6. ☐ lifeguard	f. at universities and schools

B Compare your answers with a partner.

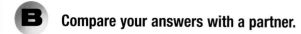

A: Where do *ski instructors* work?
B: They work *at Alpine resorts.*
A: Would you like to be a *ski instructor?*
B: Yes, I would. OR No, I wouldn't.

PREPARE YOUR SEARCH

A Look at the chart. Fill in the missing jobs, skills, and personal qualities with words from the box below.

	Jobs	Skills	Personal Qualities
1.	office worker		well-organized, responsible
2.	children's art teacher	teaching, drawing, painting	
3.		cooking, carving	hard working, reliable
4.	ski instructor		athletic, patient
5.	telemarketer	selling, convincing people	
6.		speaking foreign languages, serving food	friendly, polite

cook's helper
using computers, filing

outgoing, talkative
creative, energetic

flight attendant
skiing, giving instructions

B Write down three skills and three personal qualities that you have.

Skills	Qualities
I'm good at _____	I am _____
_____	_____
_____	_____

C Think about your skills and qualities, and choose the type of job you would like. Then choose the country where you would like to work.

Type of job _____

Country _____

D Now talk about your choice with a classmate.

A: So, what type of job would you like?
B: I'd like a job as a *ski instructor*.
A: Where would you like to work?
B: In *the United States*.
A: That sounds exciting.

SEARCH THE WEB

Go To: `http://www.|`

A Search the Web for job databases. Do a search using *summer jobs, student jobs,* or the country you have chosen (e.g., *Australia)* and *jobs* as keywords.

`summer jobs` **SEARCH**

SEARCH TIP
Try following links such as *Jobs, Employment, Job Listings, Classifieds,* or *Career Listings* in your favorite search engine.

Keywords

1. _____
2. _____
3. _____

B Explore the different job databases for jobs you like.

Summer Jobs Web
International seasonal and summer employment opportunities
URL: http://www.summerjobs.com/
CoolWorks
Work in places most people only visit
URL: http://www.coolworks.com/

C Now choose one job that you like and fill in the information about it below.

Job name _____ Database name _____
URL _____

D Now fill in as much of the following information as you can about the job you chose.

Job Name _____
Company Name _____
Address _____
City _____ Country _____
Job Description _____
Job Skills _____
_____
Salary _____

WEB TALK

 A ROLE-PLAY. **Act out a job interview. One student plays the interviewer, and the other plays the job applicant. Before starting, the job applicant gives the interviewer the job information he/she wrote in the chart on page 48. Read the instructions below.**

Interviewer	Job Applicant
Read the information your partner gave you. Interview your partner for the job, and write the answers in the chart. Use the language below to help you ask questions.	Answer your partner's questions. Use the language below to help you answer.

Questions	Answers
What's your name?	My name is…
Where are you from?	I'm from Tokyo, Japan.
What do you do in your free time?	I like to play tennis,…
How long are you planning to stay here?	About one year
What skills do you have?	I can speak English and I'm good at math.
Do you have a college education? Do you have any work experience?	Yes, I do. OR No, I don't.
What are your best qualities?	I'm patient and friendly.
How much are you hoping to earn?	I'd like to earn $10 an hour.
Why do you want this job?	Because it's interesting and exciting.

Job Name _____

Job Applicant's Name _____

City _____ Country _____

Interests _____

Length of Stay _____

Skills _____

College Education ☐ Yes ☐ No   Work Experience ☐ Yes ☐ No

Personal Qualities _____

Salary _____

Reason for Applying _____

B **Now change roles and perform the role-play again. Then answer the questions.**

Will you give the job to the applicant? _____

Why or why not? _____

News Online

- Identify different ways of getting the news
- Read a news story
- Search the Web for news stories
- Interview a classmate about a news story

BBC WORLD SERVICE   Sport

Africa & Mid East
Americas
Europe & FSU
South Asia
Asia-Pacific

Home
World News
Audio
On the Radio

NEWS
BUSINESS
SPORT
EDUCATION
SCIENCE
YOUTH
ARTS & DRAMA
FEATURES
CLASSICAL

Sport

Sports Round-Up

Bringing you the sports news, the stories and the results from all around the world.

Fast Track

The latest action in African sport.

The Story of Football

Bryon Butler explores people's passion and appetite for football.

Latest sports news and results
A 10 minute bulletin - updated throughout the day.

Sports news online
the latest sports news - from a UK perspective.

Sports diary
A comprehensive list of the big sporting events this month.

Only on the radio
Sportsworld
THE live action sports programme on the radio.
Presented by *Martin Fookas* and *Simon Hill* .

IDENTIFY

A   Look at the ways of getting the news below. Write how often you use these ways. Use words from the box or ones of your own.

Ways of Getting the News	How Often?
1a. watch the news on TV	b. _____
2a. listen to the news on the radio	b. _____
3a. read newspapers	b. _____
4a. read news magazines	b. _____
5a. use an online news service	b. _____

(almost) every day
_____

a few times	a week
(about) twice	a month
(about) once	a year

_____
(almost) never

B   Compare your answers with a partner.

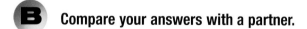

A: How often do you *watch the news on TV?*
B: *A few times a week.* How about you?
A: *About once a week.*

A Answer the following questions about university education in your country.

1. At what age do people usually start university? _____

2. a. Do you think older people should go to university? _____

   b. Why or why not? _____

   c. Share your reasons with a classmate.

B Read the following news story about a 96-year-old man starting university.
The parts of the story are labeled.

Headline ⊢

Lead ⊢

Body ⊢

It's Back to School for 96-Year-Old Man

TOKYO (Reuters) — A famous Japanese print master, 96-year-old Toyokuni Utagawa, wants to become probably the first centenarian* to complete a doctorate degree in law.

Last Monday, Utagawa found out that he passed the difficult entrance examinations for Kinki University in Osaka, and he will start his law degree when the new academic year begins in April.

"I will study for four years and then I plan to continue my studies at the graduate school," Utagawa said, promising to continue his print making at the same time.

Utagawa was born in 1903 and after finishing primary school learned the art of print making from his father. After World War II, he worked as a manager for a trading company, and then he returned to his art in 1972. He began to study at a part-time high school several years ago, and he will graduate this March. "If possible, I hope to earn a doctorate."

Already the author of one book, Utagawa lectures several times a month on how to stay healthy.

*100-year-old person

C Write each of the parts of the story (Headline, Lead, Body) next to the correct definition.

_____ This is the first paragraph of the news story. It gives the most important information about the news story.

_____ This is the title of the story.

_____ This part gives more information and details about the story.

D Read the news story again and find the answers to the following questions.

1. **Who** is this story about?   It's about Mr. Toyokuni _____.

2. **What** happened in the story?   A 96-year-old man passed _____.

3. **Where** did the story take place?   In _____

                                             (country)

4. **When** did he begin to study at a part-time high school?   Last _____

5. **Why** does he want to study law?   Because he wants to become the first _____

_____

Go To: `http://www.`

A Look for news stories on the Web. Use the news links (e.g., *News & Media, Current Events, Newspapers)* provided by Web search engines and directories.

Automobile	Home & Family	News
Careers	Money	Shopping
Education	Entertainment	Travel

SEARCH TIP
You can also use the name of a newspaper, magazine, or TV channel for a keyword search.

B Click on a news category that interests you.

Top Stories	Politics
Science & Technology	Health
Business & Economy	Entertainment
Sports	World

C Look through the list of news stories you found and choose a story that interests you. Fill in the information below.

Story headline _____

URL _____

D Now read the story and fill in as much information as you can.

My News Story

Source (name of search engine) _____

Date _____   Reporter _____

Who? _____

What? _____

Where? _____

When? _____

Why? _____

_____

WEB TALK

A PAIR WORK. **Interview your partner about the news story he/she chose.
First read the sample interview below to help you ask and answer questions.**

Questions	Answers
What is the story about?	It's about a 96-year-old man who passed his university entrance exams.
Who is the man?	His name is Toyokuni Utagawa, and he is a famous Japanese print master.
What is the name of the university?	It's Kinki University.
Where is Kinki University?	It's in Osaka, Japan.
When did he pass the exams?	Last Monday
Why does he want to attend the university?	Because he wants to become the first centenarian to complete a doctorate degree in law.

B **Now ask your partner about the news story he/she found on the Web.
Ask *What is your story about?*, and write his/her answer below.**

What is your partner's story about?

_____

_____

C **Now ask your partner specific wh-questions to get more information about the story.
Write your questions and your classmate's answers in the chart below.**

Interview Notes

Who? _____

_____

What? _____

_____

Where? _____

_____

When? _____

_____

Why? _____

_____

D **Now decide which news story is the most interesting. Explain your reasons to your partner.**

Practice Pages

LANGUAGE WINDOW

A. Look at these scrambled instructions on how to Cut and Paste information with your word processor.

> select **Cut** from the **Edit** menu
> highlight the information you want to move
> select **Paste** from the **Edit** menu
> move the cursor to the new place on the screen

B. Now unscramble the instructions. Write the instructions in the correct order.

1. First, _____ .
2. Next, _____ .
3. Then, _____ .
4. Finally, _____ .

C. Compare your instructions with a partner's.

COMPUTER PROJECT

Use your word processor to write an introduction about yourself.

1. Open a new file.
2. Write the **Title** of your introduction (e.g., Nice to Meet You!).
3. Write some information about yourself. Include your name, your age, your hometown, your hobbies, why you are learning English, etc.
4. When you finish your introduction, check the spelling using the **Spelling** tool.
5. Save your file as *YourName*.Introduction; for example, Maria.Introduction.
6. If possible, **Print** your introduction and exchange introductions with a partner.

☐ ▓▓▓▓ Maria.Introduction ▓▓▓▓

Nice to Meet You!

Hi! My name is Maria Fonseca. I am 19 years old. I like listening to music on my portable CD player and going to new movies with my friends. My birthday is on February 5th. I am from São Paulo. It's a city in Brazil. I like learning English because I like to meet people from other countries.

SHARE YOUR PROJECT

Read your partner's introduction. Answer the question.

What interesting things did you learn about your partner?

_____

_____

LANGUAGE WINDOW

A. Look at these wh-questions (questions with wh-words; e.g., *What, Who, Where, When, Which, Why,* and *How*).

What is the capital of Spain?	Madrid
Who is the Microsoft CEO?	Bill Gates
Where is Harvard University?	In Cambridge, Massachusetts, USA
When is Thanksgiving in the USA?	The last Thursday in November
Which is longer, the Nile or the Amazon?	The Nile
Why is January 1st a special day?	Because it's the first day of the year
How high is Mt. Everest?	8,848 meters

B. Now write examples of wh-questions.

1. What _____ ?

2. Who _____ ?

3. Where _____ ?

4. When _____ ?

5. Which _____ ?

6. Why _____ ?

7. How _____ ?

COMPARING SEARCH ENGINES

A. There are many search engines available on the Internet (e.g., *Yahoo!, Alta Vista*). List as many as you know.

_____

B. Choose one of the questions from the Language Window and try to find the answer using three different search engines. Then answer the questions.

1. Which search engine is the fastest?

_____

2. Which search engine gives you the most useful results?

_____

3. Which search engine do you prefer using?

_____

C. Share your answers with a classmate.

E-MAIL ACTIVITY

A. Work in groups of three or four. Write three questions you would like to ask your group.

Example

What do you like doing most on the weekend?

Why are you learning English?

1. _____

2. _____

3. _____

B. Send an E-mail message to the members of your group. On the *Subject* line write *Questions*. In the message, type your questions and leave a blank line for the answers. Then send your E-mail.

Example

Hi there! Could you please answer these questions?

Question 1. What do you like doing on the weekend?

Answer: _____

Question 2. Why are you learning English?

Answer: _____

C. Reply to the E-mail messages from the members of your group. If possible, include the message text in your reply and write your answers in the blanks provided.

D. Read your group members' answers to your questions. Write some interesting things about your classmates below.

Example

Mari likes to play badminton on the weekends.

Naomi is learning English to study in America.

_____

_____

_____

_____

E. Share the interesting things you learned with a classmate.

LANGUAGE WINDOW

A. Look at these ways to talk about past events.

He **was born** on **May 1, 1973.**
She **went** to London **when** she **was 20 years old.**
He **graduated** from high school **in 1983.**
They **gave** a concert **last year.**
She **got married** two years **ago.**

Internet English
C. Gitsaki R. Taylor
O.U.P.
ISBN 019-437226-X

B. Now write five sentences about past events in your life.

1. I was born in (*place*) _____ on (*date*) _____ .
2. I _____ when I was _____ years old.
3. I _____ in (*year*) _____ .
4. I _____ last year.
5. I _____ years ago.

COMPUTER PROJECT

Use your word processor to create a profile of your favorite famous person from page 16.

For technical tips, turn to page 68.

1. Use one or more pictures from the Web.
2. Include biographical information and other interesting facts about the famous person. You may copy and paste text if you like.
3. Include the URL(s) of the website(s) you used.
4. Save the file as *YourName*.Famous.

Michael.Famous

My Favorite Famous Person is...
Bill Gates

Name: William Henry Gates III
Birthday: October 28, 1955
Country: USA
Town/City: Seattle, Washington
Nationality: American
Favorites: Computers and Family
Family: Wife: Melinda French
Daughter: Jennifer

SHARE YOUR PROJECT

A. Work in groups of three or four. Attach your famous person profile to an E-mail message and send it to the other members of your group. Write the name of the famous person on the *Subject* line.

B. Have a look at your group members' profiles. Answer the questions.

1. Which famous person profile do you like the most?

_____

2. Why? _____

C. Share your answers with your group.

LANGUAGE WINDOW

A. Look at these traditional greeting card messages.

I wish you a very happy birthday
Hoping you'll feel better soon
Wishing you much success with your driving test
With best wishes for your future
Sending you lots of love on this special day

B. Now write a message from above for each of the card types below.

1. graduation card _____
2. Valentine's Day card _____
3. get well card _____
4. good luck card _____
5. birthday card _____

COMPUTER PROJECT

Work in groups of three or four. Create a greeting card for each member of your group.

1. Discuss with each group member what type of card to make for him/her.
2. Use your word processor to make a card for each member of your group. Use one or more pictures from the Web. Write a message with different letter styles and colors.
3. Include the URL(s) of the website(s) you used.
4. Save each file separately as *StudentName*.Card.

For technical tips, turn to page 68.

Mari.Card

DEAR MARI

Good luck on your driving test!
From Susan

SHARE YOUR PROJECT

A. Attach each card to an E-mail message and send it to the student you made it for. On the *Subject* line of each message, write the type of card you are sending.

B. Have a look at the cards you received from your group members. Answer the questions.

1. Which of the cards you received do you like the most? _____
2. Why? _____

C. Share your answers with your group.

LANGUAGE WINDOW

A. Look at these ways to talk about future plans.

I'm going to enroll in a business course.
I'll probably take a tour of the city.
I think I'll stay with a host family.
I might go sightseeing.

I'm not sure what I'll do.

B. Now write your plans for your vacation this summer. Complete as many of the sentences below as you can.

1. I'm going to _____ .
2. I'll probably _____ .
3. I think I'll _____ .
4. I might _____ .

COMPUTER PROJECT

Use your word processor to create a brochure of the school you researched on page 24.

For technical tips, turn to page 68.

1. Use one or more pictures from the Web.
2. Include information about the school (e.g., name, location, courses, social activities, accommodations). You may copy and paste text if you like.
3. Include the URL(s) of the website(s) you used.
4. Save the file as *YourName*.School.

Yoko.School

Let's Go To Kingston!

The School of English
Queen's University
Kingston, Ontario K7L3N6
CANADA
Tel: 613-533-2472

The School of English at Queen's University is over fifty years old and is located at one of Canada's oldest and best-known universities. ESL Program: 20 hours each week of academic classroom instruction in all language skills. In addition, there are conversation workshops and many other programs to improve students' conversation skills.

SHARE YOUR PROJECT

A. Work in groups of three or four. Attach your school brochure to an E-mail message and send it to the other members of your group. Write the name of the school you are going to attend and the country it is in on the *Subject* line.

B. Have a look at your group members' brochures. Answer the questions.

1. Which brochure do you like the most? _____
2. Why? _____

C. Share your answers with your group.

LANGUAGE WINDOW

A. **Look at these ways to make requests at a restaurant.**

May		a small salad with my steak, please?
Could	I have	some water, please?
Can		the menu?

I'd like	some french fries, please.
I'll have	a hot dog.

B. **Now write five restaurant requests of your own.**

1. May _____ ?
2. Could _____ ?
3. Can _____ ?
4. I'd like _____ .
5. I'll have _____ .

COMPUTER PROJECT

Use your word processor to create a brochure of the restaurant you researched on page 28.

For technical tips, turn to page 68.

1. Use one or more pictures from the Web.
2. Include restaurant information (location, food, prices, etc.). You may copy and paste text if you like.
3. Include the URL(s) of the website(s) you used.
4. Save the file as *YourName*.Food.

Chris.Food

INDIGO

1121 Nu'uanu Ave.
Honolulu, Hawaii 96817
Ph: (808)521-2900

Indigo's romantic dining room is the perfect setting for a memorable meal, with dark wooden chairs, ceiling fans, bamboo blinds along the sides of the patio, and lush, tropical plants.

The modern Asian food is dramatically presented to live up to the stylish settings—and it is excellent. Many guests choose to order an assortment of the small plates, sharing such East-meets-West delicacies as goat cheese wontons with a fruit sauce, and Grilled Asian Pear Salad with Pancetta Dressing.

Indigo's Chef Glenn Chu

http://www.indigo-hawaii.com

SHARE YOUR PROJECT

A. **Work in groups of three or four. Attach your restaurant brochure to an E-mail message and send it to the other members of your group. Write the name of your restaurant on the *Subject* line.**

B. **Have a look at your group members' brochures. Answer the questions.**

1. Which restaurant do you like the most? _____
2. Why? _____

C. **Share your answers with your group.**

LANGUAGE WINDOW

A. Look at these useful shopping expressions.

Asking for the price	Saying the price	
A: How much is this shirt?	$23	twenty-three dollars
B: It's 23 dollars.	$68.95	sixty-eight ninety-five
		sixty-eight dollars and ninety-five cents
	$356	three hundred fifty-six dollars
	$265.99	two hundred sixty-five dollars and ninety-nine cents

B. Now write the following prices in words. Then practice saying them with a partner.

1. $49.95 _____
2. $34.50 _____
3. $481.95 _____

COMPUTER PROJECT

Use your word processor to create your own shopping catalog page with two or three items.

For technical tips, turn to page 68.

1. Use a picture from the Web of each item for sale.
2. Include the name of your shop, names of the items, the prices, and a short description of each item.
3. Include the URL(s) of the website(s) you used.
4. Save the file as *YourName*.Shop.

Lisa.Shop

Lisa's Online Shop

Blue Jeans
price: $36.00
sizes: 28 x 28 – 46 x 36
narrow fit, low waist,
straight leg, zip fly,
heavyweight 100% cotton

SHARE YOUR PROJECT

A. Work in groups of three or four. Attach your shopping catalog page to an E-mail message and send it to the other students in your group. Write the name of your online shop on the *Subject* line.

B. Have a look at your group members' catalog pages. Choose one thing to buy from each catalog page and send your orders to your group members through E-mail. Then answer the questions.

1. What did you order? _____
2. How much did you spend? _____
3. What did the other students order from your catalog page? _____
   _____

C. Share your answers with your group.

LANGUAGE WINDOW

A. Look at these ways to express your opinion about movies.

I heard that | it's a great movie.
| it has cool special effects.

I really like | Leonardo DiCaprio.
| action movies.

It's | the most popular movie this year.
| a box office hit in the USA.

B. Now choose a movie and write three reasons why you would like to see it.

1. I heard that _____ .
2. I really like _____ .
3. It's _____ .

COMPUTER PROJECT

Use your word processor to create an advertisement for your favorite movie from page 36.

For technical tips, turn to page 68.

1. Use one or more pictures from the Web.
2. Include information about the movie (names of the stars, the director, the film company, quotations, etc.). You may copy and paste text if you like.
3. Include the URL(s) of the website(s) you used.
4. Save the file as *YourName*.Movie.

Peter.Movie

SHAKESPEARE IN LOVE
A Comedy About the Greatest Love Story Almost Never Told.

Winner of the Academy Award for Best Motion Picture (1998)

DIRECTOR: John Madden (II)

STARS: Joseph Fiennes, Gwyneth Paltrow (Best Actress), Judi Dench

FILM COMPANIES: Bedford Falls and Miramax Films

A young Shakespeare, out of ideas and short of cash, meets his ideal woman and is inspired to write one of his most famous plays.

SHARE YOUR PROJECT

A. Work in groups of three or four. Attach your movie advertisement to an E-mail message and send it to the other members of your group. Write the title of the movie on the *Subject* line.

B. Have a look at your group members' movie advertisements. Answer the questions.

1. Which movie advertisement do you like the most? _____
2. Why? _____

C. Share your answers with your group.

LANGUAGE WINDOW

A. Look at these reasons for going on vacation.

I'd **like to** go diving on the Great Barrier Reef.
I **like** staying at youth hostels.
I **enjoy** trying the local food.
I **want to** meet the local people.
I **really like** relaxing on the beach.

B. Now write your reasons for going on vacation. Complete as many of the sentences below as you can.

1. I'd like to _____ .
2. I like _____ .
3. I enjoy _____ .
4. I want to _____ .
5. I really like _____ .

COMPUTER PROJECT

Use your word processor to create a brochure about the vacation you planned on page 40.

For technical tips, turn to page 68.

1. Use one or more pictures from the Web.
2. Include the name of the destination and information about activities, accommodations, prices, etc. You may copy and paste text if you like.
3. Include the URL(s) of the website(s) you used.
4. Save the file as *YourName*.Vacation.

Nick.Vacation

Nick's Vacation

I am planning to go to Paris for my summer vacation. I will fly there on Air France (economy, round-trip ticket, $1,650). I will stay at the Hotel Lautier, which overlooks the Seine River near Notre Dame Cathedral. In Paris, I would like to go sightseeing all around the city and see the Louvre Museum, the Orsay Museum, and the Georges Pompidou Center. I would also like to go shopping at the famous clothing shop *agnes b.*

SHARE YOUR PROJECT

A. Work in groups of three or four. Attach your vacation brochure to an E-mail message and send it to the other members of your group. Write the vacation destination on the *Subject* line.

B. Have a look at your group members' brochures. Answer the questions.

1. What are some of the vacation destinations that the other students chose?

_____

2. Which of the vacations would you like to take? _____
3. Why? _____

C. Share your answers with your group.

LANGUAGE WINDOW

A. Look at these sentences comparing cyber cafes.

The CyberShack is more expensive than the NetHub.
WebCafe has wine, but Cafe Online doesn't.
Cafe.com has the biggest selection of food.
Cafe Connect has better computer games than Cyberland.

B. Now write a few sentences comparing cafes, restaurants, or shops you know.

1. _____ is more expensive than _____ .
2. _____ has _____, but _____ doesn't.
3. _____ has the biggest selection of _____ .
4. _____ has better _____ than _____ .

COMPUTER PROJECT

Use your word processor to create a brochure for the cyber cafe you researched on page 44.

For technical tips, turn to page 68.

1. Use one or more pictures from the Web.
2. Include information about the cyber cafe (name, address, facilities, menu, prices, etc.). You may copy and paste text if you like.
3. Include the URL(s) of the website(s) you used.
4. Save the file as *YourName*.Cafe.

Kim.Cafe

"The Greatest Coffee and The World"®
744 Harrison Street, San Francisco, California
E-mail: roastmaster@coffeenet.net
Telephone: 1-415-495-7447

Your Internet "home away from home"

Wouldn't it be nice to be able to walk into a place with a friendly atmosphere, get a great cup of coffee and a pastry or sandwich, and sit down and read your E-mail or surf the Web... even if you are not near your regular Internet connection?

San Francisco's only FREE Internet Cafe; The CoffeeNet®, (located on Harrison Street between 3rd and 4th in the heart of the South Of Market Area), offers you exactly that.

SHARE YOUR PROJECT

A. Work in groups of three or four. Attach your cyber cafe brochure to an E-mail message and send it to the other members of your group. Write the name of the cyber cafe and the city it is in on the *Subject* line.

B. Have a look at your group members' brochures. Answer the questions.

1. Which cyber cafe do you like the most? _____
2. Why? _____

C. Share your answers with your group.

LANGUAGE WINDOW

A. Look at these ways to talk about your skills, abilities, personal qualities, and experience.

> I **can** use a computer.
>
> I **am good at** | English.
> speaking foreign languages.
>
> I **am** hardworking.
>
> I **have** teaching **experience**.

B. Now write about some of your skills, abilities, personal qualities, and experience.

1. I can _____ .
2. I am good at _____ .
3. I am _____ .
4. I have _____ experience.

COMPUTER PROJECT

Use your word processor to create an advertisement for the job you researched on page 48.

For technical tips, turn to page 68.

1. Use one or more pictures from the Web.
2. Include information about the job (the name of the job, the location, a short description, skills required, salary, etc.). You may copy and paste text if you like.
3. Include the URL(s) of the website(s) you used.
4. Save the file as *YourName*.Job.

Brian.Job

WEB GRAPHICS DESIGNER

Cyber Graphics is looking for a Web graphics designer.

Job Location: Los Angeles, California

Salary: $15 per hour

Responsibilities: Designing posters using HTML. Will be working under heavy deadline pressure.

Requirements: Experience with HTML for design and maintenance of Web pages; ability to design items with short turn-around time.

Apply directly to: cybergraphics@graphicmedia.com

SHARE YOUR PROJECT

A. Work in groups of three or four. Attach your job advertisement to an E-mail message and send it to the other members of your group. Write the job title on the *Subject* line.

B. Have a look at your group members' job advertisements. Answer the questions.

1. Which job has the best salary? _____
2. Which is the most interesting job? _____
   Why? _____

C. Share your answers with your group.

LANGUAGE WINDOW

A. Look at these ways to ask and answer questions about past events.

Who was in the car?	Jack Smith
What did he do?	He crashed into a stop sign.
Where did the accident take place?	Outside the People's Bank
When did the accident happen?	Two days ago

B. Now write questions with *Who, What, Where,* and *When* about the news story you chose on page 52.

1. Who _____ ?
2. What _____ ?
3. Where _____ ?
4. When _____ ?

COMPUTER PROJECT

Use your word processor to write a summary of the news story you chose on page 52.

For technical tips, turn to page 68.

1. Give the story a new headline.
2. Use the information you found on the Web (Who? What? Where? When? Why?).
3. Include the URL(s) of the website(s) you used.
4. Save the file as *YourName.*News.

Sara.News

It's Never Too Late To Start School!

Toyokuni Utagawa, a 96-year-old Japanese print master, is going to start his law degree at Kinki University in Osaka. He wants to be the first centenarian to finish a doctorate in law.

Utagawa started working with his father after he finished primary school. A few years ago he started high school part-time and he graduated last March.

Utagawa has published one book already and he teaches people how to stay healthy.

SHARE YOUR PROJECT

A. Work in groups of three or four. Attach your summary to an E-mail message and send it to the other members of your group. Write the title of the news story on the *Subject* line.

B. Have a look at your group members' summaries. Answer the questions.

1. Which summary do you like the most? _____
2. Why? _____

C. Share your answers with your group.

HOW TO COPY PICTURES FROM THE WEB

A local Hawaii boy with roots in a traditional Chinese family, Glenn Chu's earliest memories were of a Chinese grandmother who grew her own vegetables in her Manoa garden, and cooked prodigious meals for the family in her giant wok on the wood burning stoves in the backyard. She keeps a Taoist household, meticulously observing religious practices that required certain foods for specific occasions.

A. Put the cursor on the picture.

B. Click the button on your mouse and keep pressing for 1–2 seconds until a window comes on the screen. Select **Copy this Image** *from the window.*

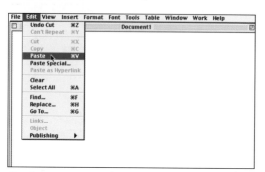

C. Go to your word-processor file. Place the cursor in the position you want the picture (see How To Arrange Pictures And Text on page 69). Select **Paste** *from the menu.*

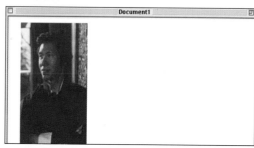

D. The picture will appear automatically in your document.

HOW TO COPY TEXT FROM THE WEB

A local Hawaii boy with roots in a traditional Chinese family, Glenn Chu's earliest memories were of a Chinese grandmother who grew her own vegetables in her Manoa garden, and cooked prodigious meals for the family in her giant wok on the wood burning stoves in the backyard. She keeps a Taoist household, meticulously observing religious practices that required certain foods for specific occasions.

A. Highlight the text you want to copy.

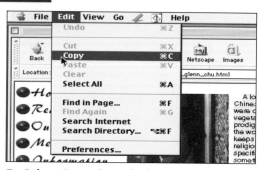

B. Select **Copy** *from the browser menu.*

C. Go to your word-processing document. Place the cursor in the position you want the text (see How to Arrange Pictures and Text on page 69). Select **Paste** *from the menu.*

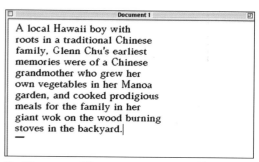

D. The text will appear automatically in your document. Remove any unwanted spaces or line breaks (see How to Format Text Copied from a Website on page 69).

HOW TO FORMAT TEXT COPIED FROM A WEBSITE

To remove unwanted line breaks, follow these steps:

A local Hawaii boy with
roots in a traditional Chinese
family, Glenn Chu's earliest
memories were of a Chinese
grandmother who grew her
own vegetables in her Manoa
garden, and cooked prodigious
meals for the family in her
giant wok on the wood burning
stoves in the backyard.

A. *To join two lines separated by a line break, put the cursor at the beginning of the second line and then press the* **Delete** *key.*

A local Hawaii boy withroots in a traditional Chinese
family, Glenn Chu's earliest
memories were of a Chinese
grandmother who grew her
own vegetables in her Manoa
garden, and cooked prodigious
meals for the family in her
giant wok on the wood burning
stoves in the backyard.

B. *When the line break is deleted the two lines are joined.*

A local Hawaii boy with roots in a traditional Chinese
family, Glenn Chu's earliest
memories were of a Chinese
grandmother who grew her
own vegetables in her Manoa
garden, and cooked prodigious
meals for the family in her
giant wok on the wood burning
stoves in the backyard.

C. *Put any* **spaces** *between words if needed.*

HOW TO ARRANGE PICTURES AND TEXT

To put pictures and text side by side, follow these steps:

A. *Insert a table with two columns.*

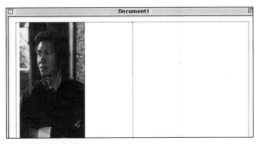

B. *In one column you can paste a picture.*

A local Hawaii boy with
roots in a traditional Chinese
family, Glenn Chu's earliest
memories were of a Chinese
grandmother who grew her
own vegetables in her
Manoa garden, and cooked
prodigious meals for the
family in her giant wok on
the wood burning stoves in
the backyard.

C. *In the other column you can paste the text you want to appear next to the picture.*

A local Hawaii boy with
roots in a traditional Chinese
family, Glenn Chu's earliest
memories were of a Chinese
grandmother who grew her
own vegetables in her
Manoa garden, and cooked
prodigious meals for the
family in her giant wok on
the wood burning stoves in
the backyard.

D. *After you paste a picture from the Web, you can change the size of the picture by clicking on it and* **dragging** *its corners or sides.*

INTERNET PORTALS

Internet portals are websites that allow you to access the World Wide Web. Most *Internet portals* have a *search engine*, *Web directory*, and other features. *Search engines* allow you to search the Web using keywords. *Web directories* allow you to search the Web by topic (e.g., Travelling, Business, Education, Shopping, News). These are some of the most popular *Internet portals*:

AltaVista – http://www.altavista.com/

Lycos – http://www.lycos.com/

Webcrawler – http://www.webcrawler.com/

Excite – http://www.excite.com/

Looksmart – http://www.looksmart.com/

YAHOO! – http://www.yahoo.com/

WHAT'S IN AN E-MAIL ADDRESS

The @ symbol is pronounced /æt/.

Period (Dot)

Type of Organization

peter.smith@mailbox.edu.au

Country Code

Username

Domain

Here are some more country codes:

uk	= United Kingdom	**au**	= Australia
jp	= Japan	**ca**	= Canada
kr	= South Korea	**tw**	= Taiwan
th	= Thailand	**de**	= Germany
fr	= France	**it**	= Italy
br	= Brazil	**hk**	= Hong Kong
id	= Indonesia	**sg**	= Singapore
my	= Malaysia	**nz**	= New Zealand